Mommy's Christmas Angel

Chris Madsen

MADSEN MEDIA

Published by: Madsen Media
Orange, California
ISBN-13: 978-0-9995500-0-7
Library of Congress Cataloging-in-Publication
Data applied for
First Edition: October 2017

MADSEN MEDIA

About the Author

Chris Madsen is a eight-time award-winning major market Broadcaster, the Original TV Play-by-play Announcer of the Anaheim Ducks and the critically acclaimed Author of the 2003 release, "Joshua Shoots! He Scores! The Greatest Call I Ever Made".

Chris is the proud husband of Lori Madsen, an Elementary School Teacher and his loving wife of over 28-years.

The Madsens reside in Orange County, California with their precious Papi-Poo puppies, Sweet Pea and Martini.

Dedication

———⟨∞⟩———

I dedicate this book to my Mommy, my angel, my "star," Cecilia Florence Madsen. Your words and actions blessed me with one of the most cherished titles ever—a priceless Christmas gift that I will carry in my heart all the days of my life. Rarely a day went by without you wrapping your arms around me, pulling me close to your heart and telling me how much you loved me…and I was just as eager to tell you that I loved you right back. I just wish we had been blessed with more days together. Now, it is my prayer Mom, that your exemplary life of generosity and unconditional love will inspire generations to live in the Christmas spirit of giving every day and to find a moment to tell their loved ones--their Angels--just how much they care and appreciate all that they do. Then, take the everlasting step to put those feelings in writing.

Merry Christmas, Mom! I love you with all my heart and soul. Until we embrace, once again...

Always,

Christopher
XOXOX

Act I

Make a difference in somebody's life...

*W*here are you when I need you, Mom? Chris thought to himself as he stood alone in front of his local department store.

A chilly breeze rushed across his face. It was a cold reminder that he had officially joined the ranks of world class dilly dalliers and last minute Christmas Eve shoppers. Chris stood frozen in the parking lot. He leaned up against a light pole beneath a flashing metal cut out of a smiling Santa in his sleigh. *Where are you, Mom?...I miss you, Mom.* With each pulse of blinking red and green miniature lights, these thoughts seemed to repeat themselves--over and over again--sapping him of his will to take a single step forward.

He took a deep breath, closed his eyes, and like taking a satisfying bite out of a warm Holiday chestnut, Chris was deliciously transported back to his childhood.

It was Christmas! A special time of year to share the love we have for those we care about most. And to Chris, nothing was more fun than holding his mother's hand, walking down aisle after aisle, store after store, checking off everything on her Christmas list in hopes of making someone's Christmas wish come true.

They stopped at a merchant's window. Chris pressed his nose on the frosty pane of glass to get a bird's eye view of a passing miniature train or an animated figure whose silent, yet enthusiastic wave of an arm could only mean one thing…Christmas was coming! What a magical time it was, featuring all the hope and enthusiasm that is part and parcel of being a kid, coupled with the love and closeness of family and friends that could take the chill out of the frostiest of days. Oh, the bliss of being swaddled in a snuggle-up blanket that had been woven from timeless threads of marvelous memories.

But that was then.

Today, the mood seemed lost.

A chilly, red-nosed Chris watched in disbelief as mother after mother walked into the store, their children either ten feet in front of them or ten feet behind, their noses buried in their hand-held devices—their fingers working more frantically than any of Santa's elves on Christmas Eve.

Where is the love? Where is the closeness? Where are the smiles? Where is the spirit?

If this is the new normal, then finding the true spirit of Christmas was going to be a far more difficult task than Chris ever could imagine.

If only I could buy that Christmas spirit in a store, he mumbled to himself as he took a stride forward into shopping chaos.

It was madness! Shoppers bumped into one another. No smiles. No "excuse me's." Only stone cold, serious looks on their faces, as though they were anxiously trying to win a race. Chris was struggling, too, as he hurriedly picked out items for family and friends and placed them in his cart. He no longer felt the genuine satisfaction that comes from giving.

Chris simply wanted to get this exercise over with.

How did it come to this?

Chris even tried to force himself into the spirit of the season by quietly singing along with every Christmas carol coming from the loudspeaker above. But what was once sweet music to his ears, especially as a child, had now been reduced to worn out words and melodies.

Who am I kidding?

Overwhelmed by the feeling of just wanting to leave the place, Chris approached the checkout line. Immediately, the woman in front of him caught his eye. She appeared to be even more stressed and pre-occupied than he was. She counted on her fingers with every item the cashier rang up. When the total appeared, the woman leaned over and quietly whispered to the cashier, "I'll have to put a few things back. I just don't have enough money."

Without hesitation, as though someone or something had given him a nudge from behind, Chris leaned in and whispered to the cashier, "Put it on my tab."

Startled, the woman exclaimed, "Are you serious?"

"Absolutely," he responded with an sheepish smile and a shrug of the shoulder, adding, "Merry Christmas!"

She extended her arms and embraced him with all her might. Chris was pleasantly caught off guard. It was the heartfelt embrace any child would immediately recognize as a hug that could only come from someone in tune with their motherly instincts, a soulful sensation sincerely laced with love and deep appreciation.

Once the woman let go, Chris stepped back, exhaled quickly and then inhaled deeply. For the first time in a very long time, his lungs felt full, his breathing was easy, and warmth engulfed him. He had inhaled a hint of a once familiar spirit whose precious gifts had left him long ago!

Chris and the woman gathered their Christmas shopping bags filled with holiday treasures and walked out of the store together.

When they reached their cars, the woman turned to him and added, "I noticed earlier that you were singing with the Christmas music."

"Yeah," a somewhat embarrassed Chris chuckled while nodding his head in agreement.

"You're blushing," the woman noted. "You have a beautiful voice. And then, you do this for me...a total stranger. You know who you are? YOU are my *Christmas Angel*!"

And with that declaration, Chris's chin began to quiver and his eyes welled up with tears.

Concerned, the woman asked, "Are you okay? Was it something I said?"

"When I was a little boy, my mommy used to call me her 'Christmas Angel'. I was my 'Mommy's Christmas Angel'."

Lowering his head, Chris added, "You see, my mom passed away when I was 12. And to be honest with you, Christmas just hasn't been the same for me ever since. In fact, every day hasn't been the same since either."

Chris looked up to the skies, trying mightily to keep the tears welling up in his eyes from cascading down his cheeks…but to no avail.

The woman reached in her purse and found a tissue, gently dabbed Chris's face, and wrapped her arms around a broken man.

"I shouldn't be laying all of this on you," Chris meekly said. "Besides, it's Christmas Eve."

"No, no, no," the stranger insisted. "Please, please get this out of your system."

Shaking his head side-to-side, Chris blurted out, "I feel so cheated. My Mom wasn't there when I graduated elementary school. So, she wasn't there when I graduated high school or college either." With tears streaming down both sides of his face, Chris continued, "She never had a chance to meet my wife. In fact, we got married on what would have been my Mom's 59th birthday. I never got to dance with her at my wedding. Never had a chance to have her over to our house for dinner. There was no celebrating with Mom when I landed my dream job. So, I never got the chance to do something really special for her…to just show her how much I appreciated her and to say 'Thank You' for all she had done for me. Like I said," Chris sighed heavily, "I feel cheated. I just do. I feel cheated."

The woman took a step back, admitting, "I can only imagine how you feel. I don't know what I would do without my Momma. But what if I told you that I think you did something really special for your mother here today?"

"You think so?" Chris said, while wiping his flush face with the sleeve of his shirt.

Placing her left hand on her heart and her right hand on Chris's chest, she prayerfully noted, "You know what all of this tells me? Her gift is in you, you know? Your mommy's good heart still beats within you! You shared that with me today. What you did for me and my family," the woman continued," I will tell this story today, tomorrow and every Christmas for as long as I live. And I promise you," she said while waving her finger emphatically, "that I will tell my children to remember the kindness of a man they may never have the privilege to meet... but learn from this man and go out and be somebody's Angel—TODAY!"

Chris stood in front of her, overwhelmed and speechless.

"Sir," the stranger added, "What you did for me and my family *is* Christmas. You gave out of the goodness of your heart, knowing that there was going to be nothing really in return, other than my thanks. Now, there is nothing I can say...nothing I can do... to ease the pain of you losing your mom. But, believe me, any mother would be proud to call you her child. And in my book, you have earned your wings!"

She held her arms out and the two unlikely holiday blessings embraced. The stranger whispered into Chris's left ear, "I pray that you experience a very

Merry Christmas…this coming Christmas and every Christmas thereafter. And I pray the spirit of Jesus will ease your pain and fill your soul every day until you are re-united with your mom again in Heaven."

"Promise me this," Chris implored the woman, "hug your mom with all your might as soon as you get home, because you have no idea what I would give to hug mine, here on Earth, this Christmas just one more time."

Stepping back, while nodding her head "yes," the woman placed her hands on Chris's shoulders and looked him directly in the eye.

"Talk to Him!" she encouraged Chris, while pointing to the sky. "He does not want you to walk around in this pain!"

The woman leaned forward, kissed Chris on the cheek and softly said, in a choked-up voice, "*Thank you* so very, very much. Peace be with you and have a very Merry Christmas."

In a flash, suddenly things didn't seem so cold.

Act II

Hold dear to those moments
that have shaped you...

————— ∘<𝒟𝒢>∘ —————

*C*hris climbed into his car and gently caressed the gold cross around his neck, looked at his broken self in the rearview mirror and prayed to release the pain that had been locked in his heart with the words, "I don't know what else to say, except thank you, Baby Jesus. Thank you for this moment. Thank you for all the blessings in my life. Thank you for listening to my prayer. Please, show me the way and help me move forward."

He sobbed all the way home--tears of joy, that is.

Once inside, like a firefly attracted to a flame, Chris was drawn to the Angel atop his glowing Christmas tree. She had always reminded him of his mother, with her warm, heavenly smile and her welcoming extended arms.

What is it about the soft lights of a decorated Christmas tree that makes a dark, quiet home seem so safe, so peaceful, so soothing to the soul?

And then, Chris's eyes drifted downward to the

middle of the tree where he always placed a most special ornament. He carefully reached in, cupped the precious memory, and pulled it to his chest.

In an instant, Chris was transported back to his childhood.

There was nine-year old Chris, sitting eagerly at a table with craft items laid out before him—a project that allowed his imagination to run free. It was a Christmas Craft Fair at his family's church and the children were instructed to take an empty prescription bottle, turn it upside down and capture the Spirit of the Season by creating a hand-made ornament.

There were so many plastic holiday standards to choose from…like Santa Claus…reindeer…snowmen…and miniature Christmas trees.

But Chris had something very special in mind.

Painstakingly, he cut a small circle out of a piece of cardboard to fit securely inside the bottle cap, then layered it with a matching circle of forest green felt . While waiting for the glue to dry, he gently placed baby Jesus at the center. Oh so carefully, one-by-one Chris softly set down the Virgin Mary, Joseph, a tiny lamb at rest to Jesus' right and a standing donkey to the left. Waiting patiently, once again, for the glue to dry, Chris cut a length of metallic gold ribbon and placed it along the outer edge of the bottle cap. Then he completed his masterpiece by adding a red ribbon to hang the ornament secured by a gold star.

Chris's Sunday School teachers marveled at how he had placed five pieces inside that tiny prescription bottle. Once everything dried, he darted down the hill, eight blocks away, where he knew his mother would be waiting for him at home.

"Mom…mommy?" Chris cried out as he shut the door behind him.

"I'm in the kitchen, Sweetheart," his Mom directed him.

And there she was…the woman who meant everything to Chris. Looking relaxed in her pink, quilted night coat with a warm cup of coffee on the table, she tenderly held out her arms, embraced her son and kissed his forehead.

"Mommy, I made something special just for you!" Chris said as he reached into his tan corduroy jacket pocket. "Now, close your eyes, Mom, and hold out your hand!"

She grinned and obliged.

Delicately placing his creation into his mother's hands, he declared, "Okay, you can open your eyes now!"

"Oh Christopher, it's beautiful!" his Mom gasped.

"Do you like it?"

"Do I like it?" his Mom blissfully replied. "I LOVE IT!"

"I wanted to put an angel in there, but they didn't have one. So, you see this gold star on top here? That's you, Mom. You're my star!"

Pulling Chris to her chest, she uttered the words that would have a lasting effect forever, "Well, Christopher, if I am your star, then how about you be my angel? How about this...from this day forward you will always be Mommy's Christmas Angel!"

"Really?"

"Really!"

"It's a deal, Mom," Chris giggled as he wrapped his arms around his mother and gave her a mighty hug and a kiss on the cheek. "I love you, Mommy."

It was a though two overflowing hearts had become one... creating a spark, that ignited into a spiritual light passing between Mother and Child. This one magnificent moment could only be heightened by a profound message delivered through a whisper into her Son's ear, "Now, go out and be an Angel to others."

Chris responded with a little tighter hug, a bit bigger smile and his eyes shut as tight as they could be...confirmation that his Mommy's gift was received loud and clear. Without the need for another word, his Mother exhaled...drew a deep breath and calmly exhaled again. Chris looked up. His Mother was radiant. She was at peace.

Act III

The most precious gift this
Christmas will not come wrapped
in paper, ribbons and bows...

*C*oming out of this marvelous memory, Chris had goose bumps. It was as though that unforgettable embrace from his Mom…that kiss…that moment…was just one heartbeat ago. He slowly opened his eyes and thought back to what he asked for that Christmas. He wanted a gold Stingray bike with a leopard skin banana seat that he had seen in the Montgomery Ward catalogue. Santa was generous enough to see that he got it.

At the time, Chris wanted that bike more than anything. At the time, it seemed like that bike meant *everything* to him.

Today, Chris has no idea where that bike is. He recalled the gold paint turned dull. The handle bars rusted from being left outdoors and the seat became sun-bleached and shredded. Heck, there's not even a Montgomery Ward store anymore!

Turns out, the heartfelt Christmas spirit cannot be purchased in a store.

At the core of Christmas is the sacred, unbreakable bond between mother and child. Chris's mom gave him one of the greatest Christmas gifts ever with three simple words: "Mommy's Christmas Angel." No cash or credit necessary. A gift that time, nor circumstance, can ever dull, rust, take away or diminish. A forever flame--the light of Jesus--and the true meaning of Christmas had been permanently delivered.

As Chris gazed up once more at the soft brilliance of the angel atop the Christmas tree, he noticed through the window pane a big, brilliant, stand-alone star right behind the angel's wings. But this was no ordinary star. This star had a glorious golden hue to it. And, it was twinkling with a passion, as though it was waving its arms and calling down from the Heavens!

Chris raised his hands and held out that simple, precious, hand-made Christmas gift he had made for his mother. Despite all the years that had passed, the glue had held...the gold star was still on it, because the Craft Fair did not have an angel.

He smiled widely, chuckled in confidence, wiped a tear from his cheek, nodded his head, and softly said, "Turns out, I've had an Angel with me all along. I should have known." Chris pointed to his golden star in the sky, blew a kiss and lovingly whispered, "Merry Christmas, Mom. I love you."

To the naked eye, others in that checkout line may have seen Chris as a Christmas hero of sorts…the woman's angel. But, in fact, it was the stranger who delivered the real gift of the season. With genuine gratitude, an attentive ear, and a mother's intuition, she reminded Chris of the priceless gift his Mommy had bestowed upon him so many Christmas' ago. A mother's love lives and flourishes inside her child forever! All the goodness of a mother's heart beats inside her child forever. And, whenever her child extends a piece of their heart freely to others, the mother's legacy of love beats on, while nourishing the child's soul in its quest for inner peace.

As he placed his Mother's ornament back on the tree, Chris chuckled to himself in disbelief. Of all the ways to communicate these days, he and the stranger never exchanged names…never exchanged numbers. And yet, as sure as he was standing there, both he and she would remember this Christmas Eve, and each other, for the rest of their lives.

The clock struck midnight.

It was Christmas!

Time to celebrate the birthday of the greatest gift ever bestowed upon humankind. Along with a sweet reminder to extend the gift of recognizing the Angels--known and unknown--that touch, and bring so much joy to your life. To hold out your arms and embrace and appreciate those Angels who are generous and loving enough to share a piece of their hearts with you—making every day a gift... today, tomorrow and always, on Earth and in Heaven.

We are all Mommy's Christmas Angels.

"Now, go out and be an Angel to others."

"Mommy's Christmas Angel" and Your Legacy

A Heartfelt Letter and a Call to Action from the Author

*P*erhaps the most powerful Chapter of "Mommy's Christmas Angel" is the one that has yet to be written...the page titled *From my heart to yours.*

One of the harshest realities that became painstakingly apparent to me while writing this book was that I do not have a single letter from my mother. In fact, the only two writing samples that I have of my mom's is a signature on an elementary school report card and on a baseball from a Championship title game that I pitched in nearly 50 years ago.

I implore **everyone**: moms, dads, children, grand-parents, partners, guardians, aunts, uncles--anyone who wants to gift their angel this Christmas--to please ensure your own legacy by taking the time to write a heartfelt note on the *From my heart to yours* page, sharing why they are so special to you. Believe me, it will become one of their most cherished keepsakes ever and will take on even greater meaning as time marches on!

In fact, my wife and I and our two puppies were forced to evacuate our home during the California fire season. The first two things I packed was a hand-written note from my Dad and the ornament that I made for my Mom. Please, write to your Angel! Nothing you can buy in a store could possibly compare.

Wishing you a very Merry Christmas!

Always,

Chris Madsen

Author, "Mommy's Christmas Angel"

P.S. Please visit mommyschristmasangel.com and share your photo, testimonial and *From my heart to yours* note with all of the angels of the world. (Subject to approval)

From my heart to yours...

Mommy's Christmas Angel

"...if I am your star, then how about you be my angel?"

"...from this day forward you will always be Mommy's Christmas Angel!"

MommysChristmasAngel.com

Author's Acknowledgments

~~~~~~~~~~~~~~~~~~~~~~~~~~~~~~~~

*M*y heartfelt "thanks" go out to…

My lovely wife Lori, who stood by my side throughout this two year endeavor, while also being patient enough to correct the written words (and punctuation and tense) of a guy who talks for a living. You are my star! God bless you, Honey.

To my puppies Sweet Pea and Martini who always seemed to give "Papa" a kiss on the cheek—at just the right moment—to lighten the mood and keep me moving forward. I love you critters!

To my Dad who loved and respected my Mom with a such a passion and dedication that he left an indelible mark on my heart as to how a real gentleman should treat and appreciate his wife and how the bond between father and son can grow stronger with every passing year.

To my Nana who carried on the message of love after my mom passed away and always made certain that there were delicious meals on the table, a warm hug and a "Good night, God bless you," and that the holidays were celebrated with gusto!

To my Auntie Roe and Uncle Mort, who I gave the first draft of this book to and asked that they openly share their insights. I cannot thank them enough for sending me on a journey to search deeper within. I did...and I believe with all my heart that Mom is smiling down from the Heavens, because of it.

To the Reiniches and the Siedlinskis, especially Betty Reiniche, who became my mom through marriage. Not many kids can say that they have had TWO moms that have loved them unconditionally.

And finally, "thank you" to the moms of so many of my friends who "adopted" me over the years. In the book, I write about "someone in tune with their motherly instincts." I believe you recognized the void that had been in my life for so many years and you embraced me and made me feel as though I was one of your own. And for that, I will forever be indebted.

And to "all of the above," along with my closest friends--and you know who you are--every day with you was, is and always will be Christmas to me!

With all my love,
Chris
Author
Mommy's Christmas Angel